A DREAM FULFILLED

Faustina Falisie

ARPress
ILLUMINATING IDEAS
EMPOWERING VOICES

ARPress
45 Dan Road Suite 5
Canton MA 02021
Hotline: 1(888) 821-0229
Fax: 1(508) 545-7580

Ordering Information:
Quantity sales. Special discounts are available on quantity purchases by corporations, associations, and others. For details, contact the publisher at the address above.

Printed in the United States of America.

ISBN-13:   Softcover   979-8-89356-138-8

Library of Congress Control Number: 2024913113

A Dream Fulfilled

Once upon a time, we all wish our dream will be a reality. We have in our minds and hearts a list of what we would like to do, what we would want to be, what we would like to own, what we would like to accomplish, what we would like to visit what we would like to see happening during our lifetime, and finally, what have we gained from these DREAMS'.

First, we have to start at the very beginning. I know that at some time at a very young age, you as tiny little boy or girl, you had a "dream" or a "wish" to know "what will I be when I grow up?" With this in mind, you might have gone to your Mom or Dad and asked for an answer to this vital question that will "mold" your life and give you a dream to follow. You may ask an older family member or just state your decision. This will instill in you a "DREAM" to follow. In today's world, it has become easier to fulfill your DREAM, for anything is possible. Maybe your little boy has a state that he wants to become a "baseball player" (like his favorite idol). This is a greater path to take and it would be an amazing experience to walk him through his dream. You, as a parent, will also encourage him to be the best he can be in all his endeavors. I am sure that you will guide him to also have the necessary education that if his dream does not happen, he will have his education to fall back upon.

This is a life story of an ordinary family; Bob and Barbara Smith have two children; their son Travis and daughter Marie. They live in New York City. In a grownup's world, many of us are entangled in the daily routine of the day's scheduled duties. This is necessary for the average middle-class family in order for them to meet their obligations.

When we "rise and shine" for the day; Mom is in the kitchen preparing the lunches for the children and dad for them to take to school and work. Mom is also preparing a quick breakfast for all. The children like cereal and milk and Bob likes his scrambled eggs, toast and coffee before running out the door for their daily

1

routine. Barbara has a part-time job so she is last in line for breakfast. Then she prepares herself to leave for her four hours of work at a diner just a few blocks from their apartment. This helps in the family's income and she saves all of her earnings for the children's future education costs. The Smiths are looking ahead in order to be able to let their children be furnished with backing to give them the opportunity to achieve a better life and have their dream come true.

Travis now is only seven years old, with a birthday coming up next month and his sister, Marie is six years old and both have many years ahead of them to achieve their dreams. We all know that the years pass-by us very quickly and children have no concept of this, but they will soon cross this same bridge in due time.

It is the month of March and Travis is looking forward to "Little League Baseball" sign up day for this season. The following week, his classroom teacher made an announcement about a sign-up day for Little League Baseball and passed around a message flyer to those who were interested in joining for this season. This note will explain in detail, the date, time and what is needed for each player to bring practice. The first meeting was on a Saturday at 10 A.M. That weekend Bob made no plans and told Travis he will be taking him to the playground on this first day, Travis gulped down his breakfast and hurried his dad out of the house to be at the playground on time. Travis had so much enthusiasm that he could not sit still in the car and said; I just cannot wait till we get started. The coach happens to be Travis' classroom teacher and was glad to meet his dad. The coach was Mr. Kelly and Travis introduced his dad to him. After signing up, the boys were given instructions as to the importance of weekly practice and were told that any absence or lateness is not acceptable. The coach told the boys that he expected them to be there for every practice to build a strong team. There would be after school practice every Wednesday for about two hours and every Saturday morning from 10:00 AM till noon. Attendance was mandatory for all for the entire season. While Travis was excited about this, his dad was thinking ahead and hoped he did not have work on Saturdays. Mr. Smith's work schedule sometimes kept him late in the evenings when he would have to pick Travis after work on Wednesdays. He will make arrangements with Barbara to cover him if he had to work late at the office. When someone makes a commitment to be there for Travis it will have to be done. Travis was given a list of things to bring to school for next Wednesday's practice. He was really excited and looking forward to the following week.

When Travis arrives home, he was bursting with enthusiasm about starting his first Little League baseball season. He ran over to his mom and went through the great feeling he had. He immediately asked his mom, "what if dad cannot take me on Saturday to practice, do you think you can so I will not miss practice?" Mom answered Travis quickly and reassured him that she will definitely do that for him. Travis began jumping with joy and hugged and kissed his mom at least four or five times. Travis thanks his mom over and over, again and again. Now, he was told to get his homework done and be ready for bed by eight o'clock.

His mom said: "you know an athlete needs his good sleep". Travis did as mom told him and he completed his homework in twenty minutes, got his pajamas and ran to shower up for the night. He still was so excited, that he could hardly get to fall asleep and once again loudly thanked his mom and dad shouting from his bedroom. That evening Marie was very quiet and went into her room and readied herself for bed. Mom took notice of this and she had a long talk with Bob that evening on what she noticed about Marie's attitude before she went to bed. When Bob and Barbara sat down to watch television, she spoke with her husband about how Mari was acting and explained to him that she noticed that Marie seem a little ignored because Travis was getting all of that evening's attention from them. She said; "I think we have to do something for Marie too. Bob agreed and suggested to have Marie go to a dance or music class. Barbara thought about this and suggested that she will talk to Marie about it. The next morning, at the breakfast table, Marie sat with her head in her hands and looking quite sad. She suddenly looks up at her mom and asked: "what will I be when I grow up?" Mom turned to Marie and told

3

her; "she can be anything she wanted to become." Marie quickly replied to her mom and said; "I think I want to be a Ballerina". Her mom told her that would mean many years of dance lessons and lots of serious practice, do you think you can handle this? Yes, mom replied Marie. OK, I will get some information from my co-worker, she has a daughter taking dance lessons for the past few years and may lead us to a good dance studio. I can take you on Saturdays too when I drop Travis for his baseball practice and we can head on to your lessons. With this Marie gave her mom a big smile and opened her big blue eyes wide, expressing great excitement and she hugged and kissed her mom and told her how glad she was about going to dance classes. Now the Smith family are involved in their children's ambitions and after school activities and will do everything possible to let them achieve their "DREAMS". The after-school baseball meeting began with the entire group of players getting together for their first tryouts for the Coach to see where he would like to place each player. The Coach was watching each player to find their strength executing each play in order to play them in the best position where they would be the most value for their team. The coach lined up the boys a few feet apart from each other and had them fielding ground balls, fly balls, and some direct faster throws to see who was able to catch and return the ball to him. The players that were able to catch the fast ground balls were placed in the infield. The first groups were assigned to first, second, third base and shortstop positions. Travis was asked to be the shortstop for the team and he was really happy with this. He ran to the coach and said; "I want to be as good as my favorite player, Jeter, of the New York Yankees." The coach told him he will have to practice really hard and very dependable to follow in his favorite player's footsteps. The other boys were placed in the outfield because they had good running speed and caught the "sky-high" fly balls which the coach batted out to left-field, center-field, and right-field. There were some players left to back up and the coach assured the boys that each player will get in the games for their position to replace the others during the game.

The coach had three boys picked to be the team's pitchers at 4:30 pm on their first practice day the boys were reminded that this Saturday morning at 10:00 am sharp was another practice date. While the team players gathered their belongings, their parents arrived to take them home. Travis could not stop telling his dad all that he had done and that he was placed in his favorite position as a shortstop for the team. Dad told Travis that was "great" and now he will have to be really good in that position because it was a very important spot in the field. He told Travis that he will practice with him whenever possible.

An Important Day

Today is the first Saturday practice. Travis woke up early and his only concern was that his dad would take him as early as possible for a quick practice before the teams' meeting. While Travis was dressing, he heard his dad in the kitchen and was very happy that they could have an early breakfast and set out to get to the ball field early enough for some pre-meeting practice with his dad. Travis asked his dad if they could leave soon so they would have a pre-meeting practice before the team arrives. I would like some pointers before the practice. They left home about forty-five minutes early and that made Travis happy and anxious to get extra practice. Travis took his position at "shortstop" and his dad told him to keep his eye on the ball and try his best. His dad told him to make sure when the ball hits his glove, he should cover the ball with his bare hand to make a sure it stays in the glove and be ready to throw the batter out quickly before he gets to first base. They only practiced ground balls so that Travis this is a good lesson for Travis to learn so that he could improve his fielding with every ground ball he can handle. Travis was quick, alert and caught every ball that came near him. Mr. Smith was proud of how Travis practiced and complimented him for doing so well at their first practice. Now it was time for the coach to start the coach to start the team's meeting and he had the boys take their positions in the field. The coach batted the ball to each player and taking notice of the boys' skills and he coached each one on the correct way to catch the ground ball or fly ball that was batted to them. He paid close attention to the infield players as they had a very important position. He watched Travis at shortstop and gave him special instructions on his fielding. After practice, Travis and his dad went over some pointers.

During the time that Travis had baseball practice, his mom and sister had an appointment at the dance studio. Marie too was anxious to begin dance lessons, but today was only to schedule her for the following week in a beginner's class. When the family gathered together, they could on talk about their exciting day.

Mom made arrangements for Marie's dance classes which will begin the following Saturday morning. This schedule worked out perfectly; dad would take Travis to baseball at ten A.M. And mom will bring Marie to dance at 10:30 A.M. every Saturday. Everyone was happy with the time schedule for "little league baseball" and "dance classes".

Now months of practice and lessons have passed by and Travis and Marie are enjoying and learning new techniques every day. Travis is getting better and better with every game. Marie is getting to enjoying her dance classes and she too is improving every week. Dad and mom now have these new events to attend and are enjoying their children's enthusiasm at baseball and dance.

The first season was just "great", as Travis team won almost every game and finished in second place. Marie's dance lessons were getting harder and harder for the little five-year-old but she is hanging in there and doing her best and having fun. It is the end of summer and baseball for this year has ended and Travis if ready for the new school year. Marie is looking forward to starting in first grade this year. She will continue dance classes on Saturdays and is looking forward to learning the new dances for her first Christmas Dance Show which will take a place in a few months.

Travis will always be involved in his school sports and he too is looking forward to next year's baseball season. He and his dad still go to the park and Travis keeps practicing scooping up the batted ground balls when they practice in the schoolyard or at the parks' field. Travis loves these practices with this dad and he is learning more and more new techniques and is becoming a real good shortstop player. His dad keeps reminding him that "practice makes perfect" in anything you do.

Three Years Later

Now summer has gone by and it is September and the first day of school and the Smith family are excited about the beginning of the new school year. This New Year will come upon the Smith family with many changes. Marie will be starting a new schedule in the fourth grade and is looking forward to meeting again with some of her friends and classmates. Travis is now in Middle School and will take the bus and meet new classmates. Mom will be walking Marie to her school just three short blocks from home. Bob and Barbara also leave for work after the children are dropped off. Barbara's workplace is just a few blocks passed Marie's school, so after walking her there she leads for the Diner where she works part-time till 3:00 P.M. today is the first day on the Smith's new daily routine schedule. It is great to have the children get involved in after-school activities but it does entail reorganizing a new schedule for everyone. It is like putting in a half days' work before leaving the house every morning. Most of the chores are done by Mom (that is why we are known as "Super Mom"), and then everything falls into place on a daily basis. Now it seems like "all is well" and the day has begun. The children are at school, Barbara is at work and Bob is headed for his office and before starting work he gives his mom a call to check and see if she is OK. Monday and Tuesday are normal days, but Wednesday Travis attends after-school activities and Bob has to pick him up after work. Marie and mom are at home and she helps Marie with her homework. After that is done, mom starts dinner for that evening. Bob meets Travis at the school and takes him home. Travis does his homework while waiting for dinner. Everyone had a busy day and now they can finally relax, have dinner and talk about their exciting day. Marie made a new friend, her name is Sara, and she lives just one block from their home. We know what mom has done all day and to say the least, it was a hectic day. Travis started in a new school this week and has met new friends and a few boys that played baseball with him in "Little League". He likes the new school and teacher and is looking forward to getting involved in some after-school activities. Wednesday will be Travis' first practice day and he will stay in school till practice is over. There have been a few changes starting with a new coach for the seasonal game program which involves all sports. While weather permits, they will play some baseball outside during September and October and then basketball for a few months too. This disappointed Travis because he thought it would be baseball only.

After dinner, Marie told her parents she had a very busy school day and the day was very long and tiring. She felt really exhausted and went to get ready for bed. Now Bob and Barbara had time to relax and unwind from their busy day too, but they were happy to have at least a few hours to talk to each other before starting the next day's routine all over again. Thursday and Friday are less hectic than Wednesday and Saturday. Saturday is dance lesson day for Marie and Bob takes Travis out to the playground for some baseball practice. The days are becoming easier to handle as the children are getting into their scheduled routines.

Years Later

Travis now almost eighteen and graduating high school this year and Marie starting her first year in high school. Season after season Travis has become a real good ballplayer. He has been on the high school baseball team and played regularly throughout every year and has improved his game tremendously. This will be his last year in high school and he is playing like a real "champion". During one of the games against another high school team Travis played his best baseball game ever and at this game, a "baseball scout" was keeping a close eye on Travis. During his game, the coach was called over by the scout and he questioned what plans doe his out-standing shortstop player have for the next year? The coach was asked by the scout to arrange an appointment with Travis to talk to him. After the game, he gave Travis the message and set down to talk to him. This day Travis played his best game ever and he got three hits; with one being a home run sent out of the ball field. The coach was delighted to have Travis get a break he so well deserved and he was just as happy as his shortstop to give him the good news. Travis had a very special day and could not wait to share the "good news" with his dad (who had to work) at his office; so, he called him and asked him when would he be able to meet the scout. His dad replied: "I will be there anytime necessary, just make an appointment and let me know." This was a very special day for Travis and his family.

Travis had a very special day and could not wait to share it with the family. In the evening of this eventful day, the focus was on Travis as he went through his exciting day. Dad reminded Travis that college was the first and most important decision that had to be considered by him. Mom sat back and let Bob discuss the "pros" and "cons" that Travis had to take into his consideration. They all knew that a college education was very important for his future. Travis wanted the opportunity to become a major league baseball player or at least try it out. He promised his dad that if it didn't work out, he will definitely attend college.

This was the "BIG DREAM" for Travis and he wanted to pursue the change of a lifetime to fulfill his ambition in baseball.

High School Graduation Day

His High School Graduation was great. Travis received honors and was among the top ten graduates. At his graduation party all his friends, relatives and team-mates congratulated Travis on his great school year and for his outstanding achievement in being chosen to join the triple-A Yankee baseball minors. Now Travis at eighteen is focused on his dream and is very dedicated to making it a reality in becoming a major league player.

Through the past years Bob focused on his son's baseball ambitions and now he will have to sit back and pray for the best. Barbara still has Marie taking dance lessons every Saturday, so she will be kept busy as usual. During this year it seems like Marie has lost some interest in her dance lessons. At this time, Marie asked her mom if she would be disappointed if she would stop taking dance? She stated that she thought it is time to concentrate on her school academics and she has changed her mind in becoming a "ballerina". Mom said: "we will discuss this with dad sometime after dinner tonight. Marie now fifteen is an excellent math student and has changed her mind in order to concentrate on her future path of study to prepare for college. That evening, Marie discussed what she would like to study to follow her "DREAM". She explained to her parents that she had a desire of someday becoming an "Architect" designer like her grandfather. Marie said that her best subjects are math, science, and drawing and have an interest in designing a "sly-scrapper" that looks like it is reaching into the sky and look beautiful among all the other great buildings in New York City. Her parents listened to her describe with much enthusiasm and were amazed at her decider able ambition. Dad took a deep breath and said he was very happy with her choice of career to follow. He did explain to Marie that it was a very difficult "ladder to climb" and she would have to study and work hard throughout high school and college to achieve her dream. Mom too was very happy with her decision and hugged her dearly to acknowledge approval of Marie's choice of career for her future.

Although Marie is just beginning high school it was a smart idea to play ahead. Just one final word – Bob said; "we think you have made a wise choice, but you will work hard and study hard to make you 'DREAM' come true. Now with this having all been said and done, Mom said it is time for after dinner dessert; how about some piece of ice-cream for everyone? Of course, everyone was in favor of this. Marie said she was calling Granny and letting her know my school plans.

Mom and Dad's concern was: how to start saving for this college tuition? Naturally, we can plan so much but before you know it, it is upon you.

This was an exciting year for the Smiths; Travis graduating High School, his acceptance to join the baseball training camp to pursue and hopefully fulfilling his "dream". Now, Marie (in a very grown-up way) making a decision to follow her dream by choosing which college degree she hopes to follow to make her future secure and fulfilling too. Bob and Barbara will have to be as supportive as possible and assuring them that they will be there for them every step of the way. It has gotten late and now the time has come to end this day, try to relax and get some rest.

In between everything that has been happening, they completely forgot that next weekend was Travis's birthday and he will be coming home for a few days before leaving for camp. Travis had been away a few weeks for meetings for camp preparations. In between everything that has been happening, they completely forgot that next weekend was Travis's birthday and he will come home for a few days before leaving for camp.

The Smith's did not plan any summer vacation this year so they will have only the weekends to enjoy. Maybe they may drive to the Jersey shore on a hot weekend and have dinner out. This may be an easier trip for Granny so she may join them too. Marie will probably take her best friend Sara to have company on the beach. Travis will be away till the holidays. He is doing well and misses everyone back home.

The New School Year

The summer has gone really fast and the new school year has just begun. Marie is the only one in school this year. Travis has gone to his training camp in Tampa, Florida. Marie is starting her second year in High School. She is a good student and has chosen her major subjects and given the required classes including the second year of Spanish. The Smiths are coping with Travis being away from home for the first time of their lives. Marie came home with many new books for her studies and lots of homework too. After dinner, Marie went to her room and began her reading and homework assignments for the next day. Several hours have passed and Marie was very quiet in her room so her mom peeked in and found Marie asleep at her desk with her head resting on the last book she was reading. Mom gently walked in and woke her up and told her it is time for bed.

As the year progressed, Marie found herself studying long hours and she is becoming more mature and seriously getting into her studies. Bob and Barbara are very proud of her efforts. Marie's report card proved to herself and her parents the rewards of hard long nights of the study were worth it. She brought home a really great report and has been awarded special honors every marking period.

In the meantime, Travis called home and was glad to speak with his parents and stayed on the phone a long while. He too had good news about his progress at his training camp. His parents were equally excited to learn how well he is doing. His dad encouraged Travis to keep up the good work and someday it will all pay off for him. He was also happy about his sister's greater year in school. Travis spoke with everyone and told his parents he missed everyone and I will be home for the upcoming holidays. See you all next month for Thanksgiving Day.

The next few months passed by quickly and it is "school break" and Travis arrived home the day before Thanksgiving. This was the first family reunion since before summer. The Smiths planned a huge family get-together. They invited Granny and Barbara's parents for a great family dinner. On Thanksgiving Day everyone brought their favorite home-made dish or dessert for everyone to enjoy. Grandma Smith brought her delicious pumpkin pie and Barbara's mom came with her famous sweet potato and mini marshmallow pie to enjoy with the big turkey that Barbara has been baking all morning. Barbara announced that dinner will be ready soon so we can take our place at the table and Bob can bring in Turkey to carve at the table. Marie had to get some snapshots on her cell phone while dad was doing the carving. Everyone was very thankful for the past year with Marie's great school year, Travis's successful training and for everyone's healthy year and hopefully, we will enjoy the same for this whole year. A toast to all for a happy holiday and our thanks for this great food and family dinner. Granny Smith invited everyone to her home for the Christmas Eve dinner. The following month was Christmas shopping time so the days went quickly and before long it was Christmas Eve at Granny'. Barbara was glad she still had her parents around to enjoy the holidays together. Unfortunately, Bob's dad had passed-on about five years ago so Granny was more than happy to have the rest of her family come spend the holiday with her. Before getting to his mom's house Bob stopped at their favorite bakery and bought a box of special Christmas pastry, cookies and the Bobka Bread for everyone to enjoy with their holiday dinner. Granny is a good cook and everyone is enjoying the holiday feast. They arrived at her house and everyone had a box or dish to carry in. Granny welcomed everyone at the front door and they all had gifts and food to bring in. She cheerfully said "Merry Christmas" to one and all and hugged and kissed every single person as they walked in. This made Granny very happy and she said: "this is what holidays are about." The ladies gave Granny a hand in the kitchen and the kids set the dining room table. The men placed the gifts under the Christmas tree to be opened after dinner. This worked out just fine as it gave Bob and Travis sometime together to talk. Bob gave his mom a yell from the living room and said; "it smells so good in here that I can hardly wait to dig in". Granny replied; "good things are worth waiting for Bob and you too Travis, remember this." Finally, "all is ready". Everyone took a seat at the table and the food was brought in for dinner. Granny had prepared a great honey ham and all the trimmings too.

The Christmas tree was lit and all the presents under the tree glimmered with the reflection of the lights and made the room filled with love and happiness. Bob lifted a glass to cheer Granny for her fabulous dinner and cheers of Merry Christmas to one and all. The platters were passed around and Bob was cutting the ham into slices to make it easier for everyone to help themselves to a serving. The ladies filled their glasses with fruit punch and the others with wine. Marie was the photographer of the family and she got up and said: "don't touch the food until I get a few photos of this beautiful table and everyone in the picture". Everyone gave her a few minutes to take a few photos of the table of food and Granny too as the chef of the day. She gave Granny her present because she wanted her to take a photo in the apron and Chef's hat which she bought especially for her. Granny got a kick out of this and posed for the photo alone. She also wanted a photograph with the whole family. Photos are the way to keep and hold dearly the remembrances of these moments.

Everyone sat and started eating away and with every bite became the sound of enjoyment of the delicious and fabulous holiday dinner. "Umm. Umm, Umm". After having eaten all their dinner, they needed a break from the table to make more space the desserts. They decided they would open the gifts while a pot of coffee was brewing. The grandchildren were very happy to hear that and they placed everyone's gifts in front of them to have handy for an opening. They always let Granny open her gifts first and then Marie and Travis and then everyone else. Granny was wearing the gift from Marie and now Travis, Bob, and Barbara gave her their gifts too. It was a beautiful blue sweater and a hat and scarf set from Travis. She said these will be her favorite winter things to wear. Hugs and kisses to all from Granny. Marie was given an old briefcase (that belonged to her grandfather) and it was filled with special office tools that at one time he used as an Architect. She was amazed at what she found in the briefcase and she said will keep this forever. This was the first time Marie heard that her grandfather was an Architectural Engineer as she wishes one day to become. Granny told Marie, "grand-pop" would have been very proud of you to follow in his footsteps. She kissed Granny and was so happy to have this special gift given to her. Travis too got a big surprise as his gift was grandpop's old baseball glove and baseball cap from when he had played while attending college and he too was lost for words, he gave Granny a great big kiss and thank you and said he will treasure this forever. These were very "special gifts" for the grandchildren to have. Bob and Barbara were given a box wrapped in Christmas paper and a big red bow which contained a very special gift. Granny gave them a certificate of grand-pops investment funds which was left for the grandchildren's college education only. They were very surprised in receiving this and promised that it will be only used for that purpose. Bob and Barbara were extremely grateful for this unexpected gift. Now it is dessert time; coffee, hot chocolate, cookies, pastries and all types of Christmas goodies too. The day was too beautiful to end, but it is already nine o'clock in the evening and time to head home. This was a great family dinner and everything was so beautiful and all of Granny's food was enjoyed by everyone. Time to hit the road so hugs and kisses all around and off we go. Thank you so much once again. Drive safely kids, see you soon. As they drove away Granny waved and threw kisses to all and be careful. This was a great day for everyone and we will all sleep well tonight.

Just a week to go and the holidays are over and then back to the routine of work and school. New Year's Eve is the time to stay at home, turn on the TV and sit to watch the bringing in the New Year as the big ball drops down at Times Square. A few friends may be with us to toast in the New Year with a glass of champagne and snacks.

Today is January 4th and the beginning of Marie's new semester. She is looking forward to meeting her new teachers and classmates. Much to her surprise, her best friend, Sara, was not in class. Marie was sad about that but elated to have her favorite teach as her instructor in math. Immediately upon arriving home, she called her friend, Sara, at home and was told by her mom that she had become very ill during the Christmas and New Year holiday and had to be rushed to the hospital for an emergency appendix surgery. She asked if she could please speak with Sara and her mom passed her the phone. "Hi Sara, I missed you today in class and was worried about you", but I am happy you are getting better and will return to school by next week. Marie told Sara "get well and call me anytime.

In the meanwhile, dad and Travis were enjoying each other's company and sat and talked about Travis's baseball training for a long while Marie excused herself and went into her room to read and do the next day's homework. Dad told Travis how great his sister is doing in school and that she changed her mind about dance and now wished to major in Engineering when she starts college. That is just "great" I am sure she will be excellent in any field she chooses because of her hood study habits. Travis congratulated her on her smart decision for college next year. Dad told Travis that he was proud of both of them. Travis will be leaving the following Monday and head back to training camp. The evening ended and everyone was ready for bed. Bob and Barbara needed their rest, as the next day, was the beginning of their routine week. After a good night's rest, everyone was up early for breakfast before starting a new day. Travis mentioned that he planned to visit his former coach at his old school and fill him in with his experiences and training at the camp. Travis had a great visit to the school and his chat with his old coach which brought back many memories for him to cherish forever. Travis told his parents of his enjoyable day with the coach. After dinner, he was excited about packing and getting ready to return to Florida.

This is Marie's senior year in high school and she too is looking forward to an exciting year. Marie said "goodbye" to her brother, as he will be leaving before she will be up for school that next morning. He gave Marie a big hug and kiss and told her to keep up the good school studies. Everyone retired for the night for the next day will be very hectic for all. Travis had a left real early, even before everyone was up, and suddenly they all realized how much they miss him not being at home.

Now, the day has begun for all, Mom cooked breakfast, Dad packed Marie's lunch and his too and everyone is ready to head out for the day. Marie was anxious to get to class and was hoping that her best friend, Sara, had recovered fully and is back to school and in her class. All Marie's classmates were present and she was overjoyed in having Sara there too. Another school semester has begun and everyone was ready and willing to get started on the first day back. When the day ended Sara met Marie and while heading home they talked about their holiday surprises. Everyone had a great time on Christmas Eve at Granny's and she cooked a great dinner. When Marie arrived home per mom was getting supper ready and Marie went into her room and started on her homework for the next day. Mom was happy to see this while she continued making dinner. Travis left real early that morning and he should be about halfway through his trip and will probably call Bob in the evening. Before eating Bob said a few words of prayer and thanks for all the holiday's good fortunes and may the next year be as pleasant for all. Shortly after, Travis phoned home to let them know he will spend the night in South Carolina at the Best Western off of Rt. 95 and get going again about six o'clock in the morning, love to everyone, I will call you tomorrow night. After dinner, Marie told her mom to sit and relax and she will clean up the kitchen. Mom like that so she could sit and have the TV to herself to catch up with the weather and news reports.

The next morning, they all left for work and school. Marie walked up the street to school with her mom to meet her friend Sara and walk together. The weeks and months cannot go fast enough for Marie as she really looking forward to graduation. Next month she will be taking her S.A.T.s and hopes to do well in her scores in order to possibly be offered a scholarship when entering college for Architectural Engineering. Bob and Barbara are anxious for her to achieve her dream. The days, weeks and months are going fast.

Travis calls home mostly on the weekend for the misses everyone and always enjoys a phone visit with his family. He even calls Granny on Sunday mornings, just to say "hello" and how is she doing; she always says "better now with your phone call." Take care and stay healthy, love you, Travis." On his last call home, he was really excited to give his dad an up-to-date report on his progress at camp. Everyone seems to be doing well and the family is always glad to hear how well is doing in the sport he truly loves. He considers himself very fortunate to be a "Yankee" rookie. He has always been a New York Yankee fan. Bob and the family are always happy to hear from Travis every week as he gives them an update on his experiences at camp. He is now twenty years old and looking forward to hopefully being placed on a more permanent player's roster. Maybe with a little luck and all of his hard work his dream may come through for him. Everyone is backing Travis up and wish the best for him. The next day Travis called again and invited the family to his first game as a shortstop for the team during a spring training game. They were all thrilled about the good news and he was hoping that they could come to this game. Everyone was happy about going to his game this coming Saturday as it was a trip to Staten Island's AAA field. Bob called Granny too and gave her the good news about her grandson's upcoming game. She quickly responded to Bob telling him to wish Travis good luck on his first chance to shine on the ball field. Everyone can hardly wait till Saturday comes to go to the game. Finally, it was Saturday morning and they all were ready to go. The Smiths had a quick breakfast and then they were ready to go. They headed downtown to the ferry and then had a short drive to the stadium in Staten Island. Everyone's spirits were "flying high" and all were very anxious and looking forward to today's game. When they arrived there, they drove around for a parking space, parked their vehicle and went to purchase these tickets for the game. Bob knew he had a special window to go to and all he had to do is give Travis's name and position. He asked for tickets on the third base side and the sales-person at this window had their tickets in reserve. Bob asked the price, but these were held for Travis's family members and the salesperson said these are all paid for. This is a surprise for the Smiths as Travis took care of getting the seats for them. They all anxiously waited for the players to take the field. The Yankees were playing against the Boston Red Sox, who were up first as the visiting team. A day at the ballgame is most enjoying, especially if a family member is playing his first game as Travis is. Marie kept her eyes on Travis and told her parents how proud she was of him. The pitcher had his warm-up pitches and the game is about to begin. The first half inning was a "one, two and three outs with no hits, no runs for Boston." The first Yankee batter strikes out, the second batter slammed the ball to the outfield and it dropped in for a double, Travis is up next – he gets a hard hit double right up against the middle and now they have runners on second and third and only one out. The next Yankee batter comes through with another double and scores the two men from a base for the Yankees and it is 2 to 0. The next batter strikes out, making it two outs. The next batter hits a real "hot-shot" right back to the pitcher for the third out. The first inning ends with the Yankees leading two to zero. The second inning the pitcher settled down and strikes out the next three batters. Yankees are doing great and they seem to have some strong players and their hard practice is paying off. Yankees did not get a hit in the third inning and the score remains the same, two to zero in their favor. The Boston team lead off with a single and are hoping for more hits, but that did not happen and the score remains the same. The first Yankee batter got a single, second batter flies out and man is still on first base, one out and the next batter hits a double and they are threatening to score with men on second and third, one out and Travis is at bat, it would be great for him to get a hit now and score a few more runes. First, two pitches were balls, this third pitch has to be a good pitch and Travis is ready for it. The ball comes right down the middle of the plate Travis gives a "sweet swing" and hits a three-run homer. This puts the Yankees out front five to zero and Travis is strutting around the bases grinning a big smile as he crossed the plate and is greed by his fellow teammates with smacks on his head and high fives all around the dugout. The inning ends and Boston is up and hoping for some hits. The Yankee pitcher has a strong arm and is working hard to keep Boston scoreless. The batter coming up was hit by a pitched ball and gets on to first base. Next batter has a count of three balls and two strikes and on the next pitch he hits into a "double play". Now with two outs, the next batter hits a home run and Boston gets on the scoreboards. Next batter will face a new pitcher as the Yankee manage decided a fresh pitcher is now needed. The new Yankee pitcher comes in and puts out the fire with all strikeouts. The score is still five to one in this seventh inning. The Yankees are confident and enjoying this first game. The eighth inning ended with no additional hits; the same score going into the ninth inning. This inning also ended quickly with no hits, no run, and the game is over. The Yankees won this first game by the score of five to one. It was a great game and Travis and his family were happy with the results of this first game.

Bob called Travis and asked him to join the family for dinner. They all enjoyed the great playing of Travis and the team and they had to celebrate. Travis said he would be able to meet them at the restaurant. The Smiths told Travis to meet in the parking area by the ticket stands. OK – see you soon.

When they met, he gave them directions to a close-by good Italian restaurant. Enough with the game and let's enjoy a delicious meal. Travis asked his sister; "how are you doing in school?" Marie told her brother, she was studying hard and getting ready to take the S.A.T.s in a few weeks for her college entrance selections. Everyone was overjoyed with today's visit together and the great day Travis had in the game. They enjoyed the game, Travis's three-run homer and Yankees win.   The evening has come to an end and the Smiths headed back home. Travis met his teammates and headed back to their room for a well-deserved rest to be ready for the next day's game. Everyone had a great day as they all enjoyed the game and being together. Bob, Barbara, and Marie were ecstatic about today's experience at the ballgame and to see how well Travis played. The next day, the Smiths went to visit Granny and filled her in the exciting game that Travis played. She was happy to hear of her grandson's great game. They spent Sunday at grandma's home and she prepared Bob's favorite dinner. Awhile after dinner, it was time to head home as Marie still had to complete some homework and reading for the next day. Everyone was tired after this busy weekend and it was time to unwind and relax to prepare for the following week's work and a school. Marie took her shower and readied herself to finish the book she has to read to get a book report completed by Thursday. Early morning came quickly, mom was already in the kitchen preparing breakfast and packing their lunches. Bob and Marie started their breakfast while a mom got herself dressed to leave for work and school with Marie, and the new week has begun. Another month passed by and Marie is studying and reading to cram all the information she can for the tests coming up next week. She will be taking the tests on Monday. Marie will be glad to put these tests behind her and is looking forward to ending this school year. Mom encourages Marie and told her not to worry and that she was sure she will do "just fine". In the evening Travis called home and told his dad how well things were going. The coach really likes Travis and has him playing in every game that is possible. Bob misses not seeing his son at home and asked him to call more often. Dad reminded him to be careful and get enough rest so that he can perform at his best. Travis and the team are due for an out of town tour for two weeks and he told his dad he will call sometime after their first game. OK, have a great trip and do well, this ended the phone call.

Now, their attention is on Marie and the upcoming exams. Everyone retired for the night and the next few weeks went by quickly. The following Saturday was test day for the college entrance evaluations. This week it did not feel like the days were moving fast enough for the Smiths, so they planned a busy weekend out for all to let the time move along. It took about four weeks of waiting until Marie finally received her "SAT" scores and she did amazingly well. The Smiths can now relax; no more anticipation of nerve-racking wait for the scores to be received. Marie was relieved and felt less pressure on her. She is hoping for her favorite college to accept her. Ten days later, Marie, started receiving a few letters of acceptance and invitations for the family to visit a few colleges with Marie. Some have offered her a partial scholarship. It was one of the colleges that Marie has an interest in attending. Bob called to the college and made a reservation for them to tour the college and accepted their invitation for an orientation. This was Princeton University in New Jersey which was not very far from home. Marie will be receiving other offers and maybe better scholarships being that she did so well in the exams. A few weeks later she received more invitations and acceptance letters and one was from New York University in Manhattan. Marie also was accepted to Sanford University. The

Smiths were very excited about receiving these and soon made arrangements to attend these University's orientations. The family had time to discuss these offered and wanted Marie's thoughts and opinion on what she would like. She expressed her decision but said she would rather wait and see the complete packed offered and then decide what is best for all. Marie knew that the costs of education are quite high and it would put a burden on her parents to cover these added expenses. It was the weekend and they prepared to visit Princeton University. This was a short trip to New Jersey for their first orientation and they also invited grandma to come along. The next morning grandma was picked up at her home and she too was very excited about this trip. Granny does not go out much so this was a special day for all.

Now they arrived at the University and granny, turned to Marie, and told her to keep an open mind and take notes and think of what would be best for her. Marie stated, she is not going to decide on anything immediately and she really would like to visit several universities before she makes her decision. Granny said, "that would be the best idea". Their day went well and at lunch, they discussed a few "pros" and "cons" about this orientation at Princeton University. It was a very long day for all and as they headed home Bob asked his mom if she would like to go straight home? Yes, please was her reply. Everyone must have been too tired so their drive from Granny's home to theirs was very quiet. The Smiths had many booklets and leaflets from the University to read and discuss the Information given to them. At this time, they could not make any comparisons as it was the first of many colleges that they will visit. Everyone's busy day came to an end and they were tired to discuss anything. We will go over some information in the morning as it has been a long day.

The next morning, they were awakened by an early morning phone call from Travis. He was anxious to know how the orientation at Princeton went? Bob explained to Travis that it was a very long and tiring day and have not even discussed or gone through all the information given to them yet. They were not going to decide on anything yet because Marie has received other offers and they will take the other Universities into consideration. Bob asked Travis, "how are things going for you"? The reason I called so early was to pass on some "good news"; I have been placed at the top of the list and being sent to New York Yankee stadium as the pick for the "rookie shortstop". I am just too happy about this and cannot wait till my first game there. I am really overwhelmed with this and I hope to make a good impression in New York. Bob was so happy to hear this, he shouted out to the girls while he was still talking to Travis and wished him the best of luck. Bob told him, he knew he would make it to the top and we all want to be there. Mom to had to get on the phone and sent him "hugs and kisses" and best wishes too. His dad told him to "keep cool" and everything will turn out just fine. We have lots of confidence in you and this puts you one step closer to achieving your "DREAM". Everyone in the family was excited and happy for Travis and the "good news." Later on, they sat down with Marie and discussed their visit at Princeton. They had many booklets to go through and this took hours. Today being Sunday, they usually go to Granny for dinner so this gives Barbara a day without having to prepare to eat. Marie stated that Princeton University was really nice, but there are many things to consider. It is not only the curriculum but also the additional costs; like room and board, security on the campus and cost for each credit during each semester. We will just have to wait and compare with the other up and coming college offers.

The new week has begun the family goes through their daily schedule routine, another few weeks passed and Marie has not received any other acceptance letters from other colleges. She asked her mom; "why is it taking so long to hear from other places"? Mom told Marie, sometimes good things take longer to process than the other procedures. Sure enough, the next day, Marie received two more offers in the mail. One was a University in California, which she had no intentions of going that far from home for four years or more in college. She just disregarded that one and the school was upstate New York about four hours away from home. Marie did not want these and want to wait for some other offers. In the evening, Marie showed her dad the two offers which she received today. I guess you just did not get the letter you expected from New York University yet, but there is still time to decide. Marie went to her room to do some reading and mom and dad went through the letters she received. Mom told Bob the way Marie felt about going too far away from home for four years of college and she felt that was the first priority to consider. Then she explained to him that this would eliminate the extra costs and expenses. When school break came about, they knew that Marie would want to be home in New York City to be with Granny and her friends and family. During the holidays and spring break, she definitely would want to be here with us. Bob realized that Marie has never been away from home and on her own and that is why she feels about being far away. He is glad Barbara mentioned this and it will have to be taking into consideration. I am thinking that it will be very important for her to be comfortable and close to here. Bob had a really tough day at work today and he was going to end the night with a few extra hours of rest. This was the way everyone felt and they all retired early. Everyone is looking forward to making the right choice for Marie and her thoughts are important too. She will have at least four years of study in becoming an Architectural Engineer.

It is Saturday morning and Travis will probably call early. Bob picked up the phone and it was Travis; "Hi everyone", I am calling to let you know our training is over and we are ready to start the baseball games which will be televised from Tampa starting next Monday night at 7:00 P.M. so keep looking for the opening game. How is Granny? How are Marie's plans for school coming along? I will keep you posted on our schedule so you can watch these games. We are all wishing you "good luck" and said she too will be watching all your games. Keep well and let us know another week of work and school and still no special mail was received for Marie. She is now growing impatient and is hoping for some other college offers that she may consider. The new week has begun and the routine has started over again at home. The first thing Marie does before going in her home is to check the mailbox for today's mail and sure enough, there were three more letters from colleges for her to read and check out the details in order to make a choice to go to another orientation. This was difficult for her to do, as all these universities had many of programs she wished to take. That evening, after dinner, the family helped Marie with some decisions while going through all the information that was sent to her that day. Marie told her parents she really would like to go to New York University because it would be convenient and they would not have to pay extra costs for "room and board". Maybe I would be able to stay at Granny's and be at home at night with someone to keep her company. Mom and dad were thinking the same, but they would have to ask Granny if she would like to consider this arrangement. The Smiths had an appointment to tour NYU and then they would approach Granny with your idea. That night Bob called his mom and asked if it would be OK to visit her Saturday this weekend. Granny is always glad to have them and she invited them to come for dinner too. Dad loved the invite as he misses his mom's cooking. That evening Bob brought the subject up about Marie really liking NYU, which is really close to your home and was wondering if you would approve her living with you if she attends NYU. Granny was delighted and excited about this and thought it was a wonderful idea to have her granddaughter live with her while attending college near her home. I am really excited about this. Bob and Barbara were equally pleased and Bob told his mom he would take care of some house expenses as this would lessen the school costs. Marie was so excited about this and she hugged and kissed Granny and thanked her over and over, again and again, and kept saying "I love you Granny". This was a big decision on all and a blessing in describes for the Smiths. Marie would have granny caring and watching over her while Bob was happy having someone with his mom at home every evening. Marie and granny will be helping each other and sharing household chores. The evening ended for the Smiths and it was time to leave and return home. Everyone was happy with today's decisions and Marie was especially glad to be with granny throughout her college years. This was a big worry of the minds of Bob and Barbara; now they don't have to worry about Marie being far from home in a strange city with nobody to watch over her. The family knows Marie is a serious student and do not worry about her study habits as she has proven this with all her hard work and great grades throughout high school. Bob asked Marie, "Do you feel comfortable with today's outcome?" Marie told her mom and dad; she was blessed to have Granny both of them worry so much about her. She was more than happy and knew she is going to be comfortable at Granny's and like the choice of school that she has made. I am more than pleased with what we have decided and I am going to definitely keep these decisions which I am in favor of. I will live at Granny's and have company at night and I could watch over her too.

The next day Travis called home and asked "how is everyone doing" and "how did NYU tour go"? Bob spoke with Travis for about one hour and let him know what Marie decided to do. Travis wanted to speak with his sister so Bob passed the phone to her. Marie was really happy with her decision and told her brother, she will be more at home staying in New York City for school and especially thankful to be staying at Granny's. She offered her spare room for as long as I wish to stay there. I guess this would mean at least four years until I graduate and then I will see how things work out for me. I may decide to attend school another two years and get my "Master's Degree" in Engineering. That sounds great Marie and the best of luck to you. Marie asked Travis, "what is new with you?" and he replied; "all is going well and I still have much to learn and every day is a new experience and I am getting into the swing of things in more ways than one, I am playing hard and getting to learn what I am capable of accomplishing out on the field". I gained a few pounds and this has made me stronger at-bat as I can put my weight behind every swing. I am learning to keep my eye on the ball and be ready for the next pitch to smack it with a good swing and follow through. I am working on good batting skills to improve as a good batter. I am doing good, but I want to be better. It is getting late for me so I have to call you again in a few days, I have some plans to take care of Have a great night.

The next few weeks have gone by and Travis called and spoke with his dad to let him know that he has made plans to have everyone come down to Tampa for the July 4th week when he spoke with his dad, he let him know that he is calling Granny and inviting her to come too. He let his dad know that he has rented a house on the beach and will be sending them the flight tickets for all of them to come down to Tampa and also has a box seat for the family for the week. Travis already has called granny and she told him she was ready to pack the luggage. His grandmother was happy hearing from Travis and she is looking forward to spending another week with the whole family in Florida as they did once before. It will be great "family time" together. "OK" granny, I am calling dad back and tell him that you are happy about the invite to Florida and ready to go. When he called his dad back, he let him know that granny said she is "ready to go" so you can make arrangements to take your vacation for that week; "I will see you soon, Bye". Travis did not give him any time to think about it and hung up the telephone. The Smith family have something to look forward to for a July vacation trip to be together for the week. Bob told the girls to make the arrangements at work to take that week off. He said that is was very thoughtful of Travis to make planes for everyone to be away together for the week in Florida They all seem quite excited about this and will make arrangements at work for the week off. Marie is always doing homework, reading or studying for her final exams. This year she is graduating High School and cannot wait for the year to end. She will be going to her prom with her best friend's brother and looking forward to enjoying the happy occasion with many memories. The next four weeks passed by and this Saturday is the prom. Marie's best friend, Sara, also had a date to attend the prom at the Waldorf Astoria in Manhattan. This was a special night for the graduates and they all looked sharp. The girls wore lavender chiffon gowns with satin trim and the guys looked handsome in their dark midnight blue tuxedos. The escorts brought the girls beautiful wrist corsages and the limousine was waiting for the couples to come down; the delay was the picture taking with their parents and granny. In ten minutes, they were ready to leave for their ride to the Waldorf Astoria Hotel. On their arrival, they met with all the other graduates and some teachers that also attended the dinner. The music, the food and entire exciting evening were more than they expected and they will all have great memories of their special night at the prom. It was a great time to be had by one and all.

Just a few more weeks of school and the family will be enjoying the weeks' vacation in Florida with Travis. The next day

Travis called home and gave them an update on the vacation reservations for each of them. He spoke with Bob and gave the address of the beach house he rented for the family and asked his dad to print out the flight reservations. They will be leaving from Newark Airport on July 3rd, 11:30 A.M. on American Airlines and returning on July 10th; that is for tickers total. Travis had to keep an appointment so he rushed off the phone, "see you soon". Till then take care of yourselves, love to all. Things are going well and everyone is getting anxious and looking forward to July 3rd. They will be away for seven days and their return trip is set for July 10th sometime in the early afternoon. Bob called granny and she made a note on her calendar to remember and get all her things ready to go. She will have to bake Travis his favorite cookies to surprise him with them. It will be a busy week for everyone and they all are looking forward to this vacation.

Finally, the day has come and everyone was ready to leave by 7:00 A.M. Bob called his mom and let her know that they will pick her up within a half hour, about 7:30 A.M. because we have to be at the airport no later than 8:30 A.M. It is the holiday weekend and we have a long wait on line at the airport at check-in. I also have to park the car at the "long –term" parking area and meet all of you inside. Upon arriving at the airport, Bob drove close to the American Airline departure areas and unloaded their luggage and told the girls to go ahead and check-in and I will meet you online. The attendant looks at their luggage and placed it on their cart to have it brought in for loading unto the airplane. Bob took care of the attendant and drove off to the parking area. When Bob returned, he went through the check-in and then met the family. They had about forty-five minutes before the gate opened for boarding. Bob said: "after all this running around he really needs an as a restful and enjoyable vacation. They stopped at the concessions and he picked up a newspaper and they sat at a table with a cup of coffee and a breakfast snack. Now it was time to line up to enter for their flight. Soon everyone entered and went to their assigned seats, Marie sat next to granny and Bob and Barbara right behind them. The stewardess went through the safety instructions soon after they were on their way. This was only about a two-hour flight so they sat back and relaxed and before they knew it their

31

trip was over and landed safely. It was a good flight and they all enjoyed it very much. Travis was picking everyone up at the airport somewhere close to the baggage retrieving area. They all picked up their bags and luggage and waited outside where Travis could see them. He was parked just a few feet from the door and met, loaded his car and they were off to their beach house near Tampa and right on the ocean side. The home was beautiful, the girls went in and Bob and Travis brought in their belongings. Granny told Travis he made a wonderful choice and everything will be more than comfortable here. They all walked out to the terrace and enjoyed a break of fresh sea air and the gorgeous view of the beach and ocean. Thanks, Travis, we will enjoy this vacation. Hugs and kisses all around and granny handed Travis the box of homemade cookies which he loves so much.

Travis had to leave quickly and they will meet after the ballgame for dinner at a famous seafood restaurant. The family was all going to rest this first day. Marie and granny will share the bedroom with twin beds and Barbara will have the master bedroom with a beautiful view of the ocean. The home was beautiful and the water looked very inviting so after a rest, they took a stroll on the beach. It was 85 degrees, sunny with a very warm breeze. Granny was taking a nap as the trip got her tired out. The rest of them walked on the boardwalk and stopped for some hot dogs, burgers and French fries to hold them over till dinner that night. It will be a late dinner tonight so they brought a quick lunch back to the house for granny. They all found a favorite lounge chair on their terrace and sat relaxed enjoying the ocean breeze and watching some swimmers and surfers in the water. They all had a great day and are enjoying the "change of scenery" from the city to the beach. Marie also notice the smell of the ocean in comparison to the city air,

At this time, Travis' game had started, so Bob watched it on the TV. It was an unusual experience and Bob enjoyed seeing Travis playing another good game. He has gotten a few hits and his fielding has improved amazingly. He made some tough plays and make look easy. The 9th inning ended and the Yankees won this game by the score of four to two. After the game, Travis called

Bob to let them know that the reservation was for 7:30; I will be there in two hours, have everyone ready to go when I get there to pick you up about 6:30. It is only a short drive to the restaurant, be ready. They all were happy to have this special day with Travis. Dinner was extra special and delicious. Travis had one big surprise for the Smiths, he was able to get a reserved box for the whole family for the week so they could all attend his games. Bob was thrilled with this surprise and Travis was only too glad to be able to have them enjoy a week of baseball games that he will be playing in. This vacation will be the best for the family. Bob thanked Travis and told him to continue being successful in his position and he will have a great future. Well, dad, I have one more surprise and that is, I have been given a contract to be the rookie shortstop and I will at the stadium as a New York Yankee player within the next few weeks. This will mean a big raise for me and I am working with my Agent to get me at least a three-year contract at a good salary. Bob and everyone were overwhelmed with this great news from Travis and everyone's emotions were really high. I hope this is a permanent move for me and I hope to do my best in every game. We wish you all the best, keep your head on your shoulders and everything will work out for you. He has grown up a lot and seems to be making the right moves. Barbara too was extremely happy for Travis and gave him a big hug and kiss with tears in her eyes, she told him she knew he would make his dream come true. Granny too was emotional with the good news and told him, "Now you have the world in your hands." I feel like I am ready for the "BIG LEAGUE" I have really worked hard to get to this point of my game. Travis turned to Marie and said; "he is looking forward to her to achieve her dream in becoming a successful Architectural Engineer as she wishes to become". Marie replied; "I have a long way to go, but I am confident that it will all work out for me." I decided to attend New York University and plan to live with granny being that it is closest to her home and she invited me for as long as I want to stay while going to school. Travis, I want to thank you for the lovely place on the beach and this great dinner you have given us. I hope that someday I can do the same for all of us, love you. Will you have a day to spend with us at the beach house? Travis could not answer this now, as he does not have his schedule for the week, but I will check it out and let you all know. I will call dad and check the schedule for pregame practice. This was fun and I have to head back and get some rest for tomorrow's game. I have given you the passes for the week so I will see you all at the stadium. Have a good night and I will see you at the game. Travis had to leave, but he made arrangements for a taxi to take them back to the beach house. Take your time and enjoy desserts and coffee, tea and an after-dinner drink, see you tomorrow. Granny said; "I am getting a bit tired, it has been a long day for me but I enjoyed every minute and now I guess it is time for my "beauty sleep". Me too granny, I am getting sleepy. They walked outside and the taxi was there for them, the driver approached Bob and asked if they were the Smiths? Travis took care of this fare and I know where you are going, my pleasure to escort you home. When they arrived, granny and Marie went straight to bed, Bob and Barbara enjoyed relaxing on the terrace looking out to the beautiful ocean view and watched a few fishermen trying their luck in catching a fist or two. This is a big difference from our "city life" I find it more relaxing and enjoyable. I guess tomorrow, we will enjoy watching Travis at the game. I am going out early and get a car rental so that we can get around and go somewhere if we wish to. After breakfast, Bob went for the car and the girls told him they will be on the beach for an early swim. OK, when I return, I will meet you on the beach. I think it will take about an hour.

It was a beautiful morning; the temperature was 81 degrees and it was only 11:00 A.M. Barbara and Marie jumped into the ocean for a quick swim and granny placed her beach chair close to the water so that the waves would bring the water at her feet. Marie is really enjoying the water with mom and as turned around they saw granny getting ready for a swim too; this was fun. I did not think granny could swim anymore, but she is doing great, but close to the shallower water. We swam to her and stayed with granny, just to play it safe. Granny said; "the water is really warm and I am enjoying it a great deal", don't worry about me I am just fine." In about an hour, Bob returns with the rented car and parked it at the house driveway. He went and changed into his bathing suit, grabbed a towel and headed to meet everyone on the beach. He was glad to see the girls having their first swim and enjoying some fun. Granny got out of the water, pulled her beach chair back further on the sand so she can get dry and relax. He came down ready for a swim, he gave the towel to his mom and jumped right in between the girls. Bob could not believe how warm the water was and he too is having a good time. After a while in the water, they came out to get some sun and maybe tan a bit from the warm sun. Marie brought down a beach blanket and laid on her belly to dry off and tan. Bob sat on his towel to dry off and get some sun and just then his cell phone rang, it was Travis. "Hi son, we are on the beach and enjoyed our first swim of the summer, what are your plans for today?" Travis told Bob he could not get there today because he had an early practice and the game starts at seven tonight. His dad was disappointed but understood that Travis had to do what he had to do. Bob let Travis know that he rented a car for their convenience so don't worry about making any further traveling arrangements for us. I think everyone wishes to come to your game tonight; we do not want to waste the reserved box seats, see you later. Mom, Travis was concerned with you being out late tonight, will you be OK with going to the game? Granny replied; "I am here on vacation so I will definitely enjoy all that I can especially watch Travis at the ball game". The plans were settled and they will all be going to the Stadium. It is almost 2:00 P.M. So we should clean up and dress soon and we will have time for a late lunch at the ballpark. The Smiths got themselves ready and were soon on the way to the ballpark. Just as they got in their car there was a heavy downpour of rain and Bob hoped this would not last long for it could cancel tonight's game. I don't think so Bob that is the way it is in Florida, it is only a quick shower which is good to cool down the hot day. Sometimes, you could be standing on one side of the street in heavy rain and across the road, it would be dry with no rain at all. Granny said: "I think they call it Tropical rainfall." I really do not mind the rain down here because it cools down and clears up quickly. I know we are on vacation but we cannot do much about it. In about ten minutes, the rain stopped completely and the sun came out again. This is a great mom, you must have been praying for the rain to stop. I am happy it did, as we have a walk from the parking area to our seats. It is going to be a great day as they walked to their box seats with big smiles and grins on their faces. Bob repeated; "yes, it is going to be a great day." The attendant walked them down to their seats and before they could sit, he had to wipe the seats dry. Bob thanked him and gave him a tip. The attendant said; thanks, Mr. Smith. Bob wondered how he knew his name? Travis is a friend of mine, and I am pleased to meet his family, enjoy the game. Travis gave a glance at them as he jogged out toward his position. Granny threw him a kiss (for good luck). This is a special treat for all and they are ready to enjoy the game. Bob asked if they were ready for lunch? Marie said; "of course". Bob and Marie went to pick up five boxed lunches and for large cold drinks. They bought everything that the girls liked and now they were ready to enjoy the game and lunch together.

The first three innings were played and still no score. Bob said this game is a pitcher's duel, as both pitchers are very aggressive and are throwing a good game. That is fine, we are still having a great time watching Travis play and being down here on this beautiful day. Granny is doing fine and enjoying the family outing. OK, granny – keep an eye on the batter; Travis is up and he looks anxious at the plate. The first two pitches were balls, but the third pitch came right down the middle of the plate and Travis was ready for it and with a strong swing he sent the ball out and over the fence for a home run. This gave the Yankees, one to nothing lead and everyone jumped out of their seats and cheered Travis home. Bob said proudly, "that is my boy". This made it more exciting for the fans and the Yankees. This woke everyone up at the ballgame. The next few innings were played with only a few infield hits and all were easy outs for both teams. Now in the 7th inning, it was break-time and the girls walked up to the restroom with Granny. They brought back some ice-cream which was granny's treat for all. We are having a nice time and I needed the short walk for exercise and this is fresher air than I usually get back in New York. The game was ready to start again. Now in the eighth inning, the Yankees came up with two more runs, bringing the score to three to zero in their favor. In the ninth inning nothing happened, the game ended and the Yankees won three to nothing. Bob called Travis on his cell phone and asked if he had plans or would he like to join them for dinner? Not really, I will join you, I will meet you at the beach house as soon as possible. Bob said;

"this was a fabulous day. I am having so much fun, I do not want to think about going back home in three days. I guess the odd adage is right; "time flies when you are having fun". The next day everyone wanted to spend the day at the beach, stop for lunch, browse through the souvenir shops and take a relaxing walk in the sun. Bob thought that was a good idea and planned to do just that at the shore as it was a beautiful day to enjoy the great weather. Barbara was glad that Bob will join them. Barbara was hoping that Bob would say that. They stopped at an Italian restaurant for dinner and had some delicious food, but Marie just wanted two slices of a vegetable pizza that tempted her taste buds. After dinner, they strolled on the main avenue to shop for a few gifts and browsed through a few other shops. Marie bought a gift for her best friend and a new bathing suit. Mom liked a seashell necklace and a Florida blouse, and granny picked out a new pair of sunglasses and a cooking apron and Bob paid the bill for everyone. While walking down the street, Barbara said; "I cannot believe that we only have Friday and Saturday left before we head back home. We are enjoying ourselves, so much, and did not realize our vacation is coming to an end. We will make the most of the next two days for we will be back to our routine schedules before we know it and we have to wait till next year for our next vacation. Tomorrow is Friday and it will be the last game for Travis to play while we are here in Florida. Granny said; "I know Bob will definitely want to see Travis play again while we are here, but this game will be at night so we can do something else earlier during the day. Marie thought for a minute, and quickly said; "we really need more beach and ocean swimming, I do want to wear my new bathing suit while we are in Florida." I would like to spend the full day at the ocean and relax on a beach towel to soak up more sun to get a better tan before we head home. Maybe we can take a boat tour and see some sights? Yes, Marie, I think granny would also enjoy a sightseeing tour, I know I will enjoy that too. That night, at dinner, Barbara asked Bob, what his plans were for tomorrow? Well, girls, I am going where ever you girls plan to go and I will be with you all. Great dad, we were really hoping you would be with us for the day and not go to the ballgame. OK, I will join you girls for the day's outing in whatever you plan. What are your plans? Early morning, we can take the two-hour tour and when we return let's hit the beach, how does that sound dad? After being on the phone an hour or more, Bob finally was able to book a tour with a luncheon aboard while touring. The reservation was made for tomorrow. The boat leaves from a Tampa area dock at 10:00 A.M. and will be out till 3:00 P.M. Sounds great dad, I think granny will enjoy the breezy boat-ride, the sights to see and the luncheon aboard. She will probably love being on the ocean and it is far different from being in the city all of the time. It sounds like a great trip for the day and hopes we will beautiful weather to enjoy the day. The night ended and it was time to turn-in early and they went to bed by nine o'clock. Bob and Barbara like to end their day by relaxing on the terrace with a glass of wine and a small snack. They enjoyed listening to the ocean water hitting against the rocks and making a big splash sound. Bob said; "this vacation is really spoiling us and we will miss it all in just a few days." What time is our flight back home on Sunday? I believe we have a 2:00 P.M. flight out from the airport and we should arrive at Newark Airport about 4:10 P.M. I will be leaving the rented car at the airport here as those are the arrangements, I made with them. We will have to stop for dinner and some groceries for us and mom too. I think we had a perfect week and we all enjoyed this vacation, "Yes Bob, everything went just fine, and thanks to Travis for the great accommodations and beautifully planned week. Well, I guess it's time to hit the sack, so we can get up early for the boat trip. The next morning everyone was up early and had a delicious breakfast that granny made. They cleaned up the kitchen and readied themselves for their boat tour. Granny and Marie were the first ones ready to go and we're looking forward to this trip. Bob and Barbara too were soon ready and within an hour they left to drive to the boat dock. There was quite a crowd picking up their reserved tickets but the line moved fast. Everyone boarded the boat and made their way close to a window so that they could see clearly on the tour. Within an hour, it was time for the boat to depart. It slowly pulled away from the dock and granny and everyone is looking forward to another beautiful family day. The boat toured along the coastline and the guide pointed out the historic and interesting sites along the way. It was another beautiful day and granny put on her new sunglasses to keep the sun from blocking her vision. The trip will take several hours and at noon they were asked to find a table for lunch was ready to be served. Granny could not eat much because she was feeling a bit dizzy so she just had a cup of tea and toast and was hoping she would not be seasick. Bob was concerned and asked if she was OK. Yes Bob, no problem I am not used to being rocked. They all laughed and granny said; "I will be fine." Marie sat close to her granny and kept a close watch on her. It was a four-hour trip, two hours going out and their turnaround brought them back to dock in another two hours. All went well except granny could not eat lunch aboard the boat. They still enjoyed the sights and boat ride. They were back home by three o'clock as they were walking in, Travis was on the phone calling his dad to find out it will be at the game tomorrow? Bob told him that he would discuss it with his mom. Marie suggested going swimming for a few hours and Barbara told Bob to go with Marie and she will stay the granny on the terrace and watch both of you from there. "OK, I will go for a swim with Marie for a while, I hope mom will be alright." Granny said she felt a bit tired and will take a nap but she will be fine. Mom, if you need anything Barbara will be on the terrace and here for you. Tomorrow is Saturday and Travis wanted to know, if we will go to his last game before we leave to get back home, do you think you will be up to go with us?" Granny said, "of course Bob I would like to end our vacation being with Travis on our last day in Florida." Barbara thought it would be nice to go see the game on their last day of vacation and it is an afternoon game so we will not be out very late. That settles it, I will call him and let him know we will be there for the last game before leaving. Bob accompanied Marie to the beach, Mom watched them from the terrace and granny is taking a restful nap before tonight's dinner.

After a few hours, Bob and Marie had enough of swimming and sunning at the beach and they came in to shower and dress. Travis had an early game and he will join us tonight for dinner where he made reservations for us. Travis called his dad and gave him a direction to the restaurant where he reserved a table for 8:00 P.M. We will be there waiting for you, see you later. When they arrived at the restaurant, they both were parking their cars at the same time. They all entered and the hostess greeted them at the door, as she was a friend of Travis. She saved a private area table for his family and was very friendly as she seated them and passed the menu around the table. If you want anything please don't hesitate to ask, someone will take your order whenever you are ready. Granny thanked the hostess and said she was very nice and I think Travis made another fine choice. Everything was perfect, and the food being prepared in the kitchen filled the area with a wonderful aroma. They are hoping that the food will be as good as the service and the delicious scent of the chef's cooking. This brings our vacation to an end and it was a wonderful vacation week. We enjoyed being with Travis for a few outings and watching his games were fabulous.

The Flight Going Home

All good things come to an end and it was about to happen to the Smiths. After a long night visit with Travis, we said our goodbyes and prepared ourselves to head back home to New York City. Travis stayed with us a late as he could, but he too has a curfew and has to be back for a certain time. Sunday morning everyone was up early. Coffee and breakfast were prepared by Barbara and then a quick cleanup of the house. Bob and Barbara enjoyed their coffee on the terrace and took their long last look ocean and beach. It was a beautiful scene watching the sunrise over the Atlantic and it will be in their memory all the way home. They had a busy week but all enjoyed every moment. Bob feels like this vacation will pull him through his next year's routine. Granny and Marie were preparing themselves to be ready for their trip. They had a rented automobile which will be left at the airport, so Bob would like to leave a half hour earlier to take care of this. Everyone rushed around during the last hour and are now finally ready to leave. Bob and Marie took the luggage and gifts and placed everything in the trunk. They did arrive at the airport in Tampa about two hours before the flight departure time and it was getting crowded on the check-in lines to, they rushed onto the line with their carry-on bags and all went well and they sat themselves down by the flight area. Granny said; "we really had a most enjoyable week and we made it here with time to spare. The girls strolled over to the snack concession and Granny gave Marie money for a few goodies and a bottle of water and juice for Bob to have on the flight home. It was time to board their plane and everyone took a final glimpse of Florida through the huge windows. They had a quick two-hour flight and safely landed at Newark Airport in New Jersey. Bob asked the ladies if they would not mind going for the luggage and he will go get their car from the long-term parking area? Sure Bob, "we will meet you at the baggage area outside by the door and I will pick up everything at the curb and pack the car and head home." It is now about 3:30 P.M. and they only had a short ride from Newark to New York. Mom, "what would you like to do; to be taken home or would you like to get some shopping with us before going home?" Yes, Bob, could we shop before leaving me at the house, I would like some fresh bread, milk, eggs and just a for the week. "OK mom, good idea so we can give you a hand taking in your groceries and luggage for you." Driving and still in New Jersey, Bob stopped at a Shop Rite Market in a shopping plaza and they bought some groceries for the week. We got our shopping and now we can stop and have an early dinner so you all do not have to cook for today. Next to Shop Rite, there was a "Pizza and Pasta" place and they went in and ordered what they felt like having. The girls wanted pizza and Bob had a dish of spaghetti with meatballs. Everything was great and now it is time to head home. Bob stopped at his mom's house first and took in her luggage and shopping and waited until she made herself comfortable. They too were anxious to get home and unpack everything and put away their shopping. They were lucky to find a parking space just a few doors away from their apartment and this made things a little easier to bring in their luggage, gifts, and shopping. This was another long and hectic day for the whole family. Bob called Travis as soon as possible, thanked him once again for furnishing them the lovely beach house and dinners that he treated the family with. Bob told him to have a good night and be very careful, see you soon. While Barbara and Marie put away their shopping and unpacked their luggage, they also put in a wash. When you get back from vacation you also have laundry that was worn on vacation. That was enough work for this day and now it is time to relax while watching some television. They headed for bed really early as the next day was back to the daily routine of work for Bob and Barbara, but Marie has started her summer time with no school for two months and was happy about that.

Barbara asked Marie to please do another wash and fold and put the clothes in her closet during the day as she will be working her four-hour daily shift at the restaurant, "Yes Mom, replied Marie. Will it be okay to have my friend come to spend some time at home?" Marie's best friend came to visit and Marie told her all about their Florida vacation. She also gave her friend the souvenir she purchased for her. Marie gave her a sea-shell necklace and her friend really liked it very much.

The girls had fun just talking about the Smith's vacation and the ballgames, the beach house, restaurant dinners and how great it was to talk-out to the ocean for a swim and sunbathing in the nice hot sun. I wish we had more time to enjoy a few more weeks in Florida. Granny too had a very enjoyable week and we could not believe the energy she had to have fun with everyone.

A few months later it was time for Travis's big move to New York as he was upgraded to the Yankees Major League; things are looking good for both Travis and Marie. Their parents are very happy with the up and coming eventful changes for their children's lives. Travis will be in his hometown and probably looking for an apartment. Marie has moved some of her favorite clothes and necessities to granny's home as she will be starting her classes at New York University in a few days. She is looking forward to her stay with her grandmother while she starts classes as a freshman this semester.

Marie was anxious to start her studies that will mold her future in engineering. Bob and Barbara spent the whole weekend moving Marie's things and setting her room up at granny's. During their move, granny prepared dinner for everyone so that they did not have extra work to do. Bob and Barbara were thankful for this as they were tired-out by this big moving chore. Sunday night came fast and they were ready to get back home and relax before the beginning of their work week. Barbara reminded Marie to be careful getting to and from school every day. Bob thanked his mom again and had a peaceful mind leaving Marie in granny's care. They hugged and kissed Marie and granny and left for home.

When Bob and Barbara walked into their apartment, they felt a sense of emptiness and quiet, as it will take some time to get used to being without the children. Their life has changed and they will learn to cope through their new circumstances and they are as ready as they can be.

The first day of college was a very confusing day but she will grasp into her programs, teachers, classes and study a day at a time. In the evening Marie called her parents and gave them a run-down of her crazy and busy first day at N.Y.U. Barbara told Marie, she will do just fine and every day will become easier! Please put granny on the phone, "Hi Mom, how is everything?" "Do you need anything" If you do, just give us a call; take care mom."

It seems strange to Bob and Barbara to have their home to themselves. I guess many families go through this, but everything works out for the best. Bob, I am really relieved having Marie at mom's so we don't have to worry too much about where she is or who she is with every night.

The next day was back to scheduled weekly duties. Up in the morning, making lunch for Bob, having breakfast together and then off to work.

A few weeks have gone by and a call came from Travis; Bob answered the phone and was glad he finally called. Travis told his dad he has gotten an apartment in upstate New York, but not far from the Yankee Stadium. I have been busy getting the apartment in good shape and in my spare time I have gone to purchase some furniture and I had to put everything in place. I think it needs mom's touch for curtains and decorations. My apartment looks nice and new and I would like everyone to come up and visit. When do you think you can both come to visit? I will have a Saturday late game in two weeks, would you like to visit that day and stay for lunch? Bob quickly said the year I will let granny and Marie know too. The games are getting better and better, but we still need the top hitters to start hitting away! We are in the fourth place and working to improve that. Love to all and see you soon.

Bob told Barbara, "he sounded tired" I guess he is doing a lot of work himself but it was good to hear from Travis. I will talk to Mom and Marie and find out if they both would like to visit at Travis' place. Every weekend Bob and Barbara go to his mom's house and visit with them for the day. Saturday at noon Bob called granny and let her know they were picking up Chinese for dinner to have for lunch so his mom did not have to cook for everyone again. They arrived at granny's at about 12:30 lunch that was still hot and they enjoyed the day. They sat and talked to Marie and asked how she was doing in school and if she gets a lot of homework. Marie told them, "it is not homework but I have many books in which I need to read many chapters every night for each professor and this doe get a bit overwhelming. Travis called and invited us all to visit for the day next Saturday, do you girls think you would like to go see his new apartment? Granny said yes as well as Marie. Fine, I will pick both of you up about 9:00 a.am next Saturday.

Saturday arrived and granny and Marie had been ready since 8:30 a.m. When Bob arrived at his mom's house, he rang the bell and they met him with their coats on and ready to go. They are ready and anxious to go. Granny baked Travis' favorite cookies and wrapped them in a box so that no one would start eating them before she games them to Travis. Marie asked her dad; how far will we travel? Bob said, his apartment is about a half hour from the Yankee Stadium.

It was a good fast ride as there was no traffic going out from New York City that early in the morning. We are here! Everyone got themselves out of the car and Bob pointed to the big brick house about four doors away from their parking space. Bob held onto granny and they walked up the flight of steps to the door and she rang the bell and Travis welcomed them in. Marie and granny were surprised at Travis' great choice of colors and good taste in furniture. Granny said this is lovely and good luck with everything. Marie could not believe the size of the new flat screen TV. His mom too told Travis he made a fine choice in home furnishings. This is really a beautiful apartment! You have made a good choice. Granny, I usually get home so tired that I plop into bed by 10:00 p.m. How are you doing in the game? I guess okay, said Travis, I haven't heard any bad comments. Next week we start a two week on the road tour but the next game at home you will have tickets for a weekend game, how does that sound dad? Just great; I'll be looking forward to it. Let us have lunch and sit and chat a bit. I am really grateful for what I have been able to do this season. How are you doing Marie? How are your classes? Do you have a lot of homework? "Good, good, and year are my answers to your questions." Most of my homework is ready. Every professor does not take into consideration that each one of them hands out homework and there are many late nights of reading to do just keep up with all of it. I am doing well and enjoying most of my subjects. It sounds like you have put your best foot forward to keep up the good work. I really like your apartment, Travis, do you do all the cleaning? I do most of it and I have a cleaning person to keep it sparkled and when I am in New York. Come sit in the kitchen, I have bought some lunch meats and rolls for a quick lunch. Does anyone want a soda or coffee? Yes, Travis, I'll make a pot of coffee for all, said his mom. Today was a good day for this visit as Travis has a night game and does not have to leave until 4:00 p.m. Bob said, "I am happy for you and how fast you have grown-up and you are doing great." This was a pleasant visit and it is time for us to head home. Good luck with your game tonight, I will be watching you on TV! Granny hugged Travis and said goodbye and they all left so that Travis had enough time to get ready and leave. See you guys soon, bye.

The Smith's headed home, the first stop was to take granny and Marie home and then Bob and Barbara would head home too. Barbara asked Bob to stop at the grocery market for a few items.

New School Year

Beginning of new school year Marie was anxious to start her second year at N.Y.U. she has about ten days before school, so Barbara took her shopping for some new clothes, shoes, and coat. She took Marie home to Granny's house and they all liked the new fashionable outfits that Marie picked out. She called her friend and gave her a run-down of her new outfits for school. They enjoyed their phone visit and Marie told her friend she would like to come to visit her before school starts. Her friend invited Marie to have lunch together, the following Sunday. Marie asked her Mom and of course, Barbara said yes! Bob and Barbara went home and they suddenly realized the house is very empty without Travis and Marie. It is going to take some time getting acclimated to this new family situation. Marie will have at least three more years of college and Travis has his own apartment and now Bob and Barbara feel quite alone. We will have to make "phone-call visits" with the kids so we could know that all is well with them! It now seems like the days quickly end and the evenings pass by slowly; Bob said Barbara felt it was really different without the children being home! The school year seemed as though it just started and now it is almost summer again. This is another year to enjoy another vacation!

Travis is now in New York, but this does not mean we cannot go back to Florida and enjoy the warmer days, the beach and have fun in the sand and sun! That evening Bob came home from work and surprised everyone with a special "Caribbean" vacation package for the girls. I had a vacation fund this whole year and I saved enough for us to enjoy another beautiful vacation. I am taking you, Marie and Granny to the Bahamas for seven days; is that "OK" with everyone? Yes, Bob should have asked Granny if she thinks she can handle another big vacation? I am sure she will and this is a birthday gift to her as Granny will celebrate her seventy-fifth birthday during that week. We will leave on the day of her birthday, and she will be happy to get out of the city for one week. She really had a great time last summer in Florida!

Tomorrow is Sunday so when we go there for dinner, I will tell her to pack her bags again for a special birthday and summer week vacation in the Bahamas! I think she will really be surprised. Barbara this is a special gift for Granny as she does help us all year round with taking care of Marie during the school year! The next day was Sunday, and Bob will surprise his Mom at dinner with his vacation gift for Granny. As the day went by, Bob put the vacation reservation under his mom's cup while she was busy in the kitchen making a pot of coffee and getting some mode-made cookies for dessert. She came to the dining room with the coffee pot and sat down to end her meal with coffee and cookies, and she noticed an envelope at her place and said: "what is this"? Bob said, "just open it". When she did, she was really surprised in reading about the flight and hotel gift for her in the Bahamas. Bob asked, "You think you can take another week on the beach?" Of course, Bob, thank you so much! I was wondering if we have any plans for a summer vacation. Thank you both. I'm sure we will all enjoy this trip. I see it is for the last week in July. Marie are you ready for this? "Yes Granny, I am always ready for Sun at a beach anywhere we go." The Smiths will enjoy another great vacation at the beach! Their reservation is from July 21st through July 28th so everyone has about three weeks to buy what they want to pack and take it with them.

It is about time for us to get home so that we can get ready for our work week. We will say good-night for now and head home. Marie is spending this week at home with us; she wants to be with her friend Sara. Mom, you have a great night and I will call you at lunchtime tomorrow. The Smiths left Granny and drove home downtown. I am glad Mom was happy with her gift. She really deserved a week of rest with us.

The next morning Marie was up early and she made breakfast for all. Barbara was surprised when she walked into the kitchen and found Marie making coffee, toast, and eggs for everyone. Marie, you made a great breakfast for us. I guess Granny has taught you well and thanks for making the start of another week much easier for me. Thank you, Marie. Mom and I am really happy at Granny's, she tells me old family stories and has taken out many family photographs when Dad was a little one. I love the stories of forty to fifty years ago too.

Marie, I will be home about three-thirty see you later! You and your friend, Sara, enjoy the day. It is starting to get really hot in the city so they turned on the air conditioner while talking and watching television. How are you doing in school, Sara? I feel a bit confused in two of my classes. I really do not like math, but I passed with a fair grade. I only have to take one more year of math and I will change to the language, as I did really well in it. I would not mind becoming a teacher in Spanish. It is a primary second language anywhere you work. I would love to be a translator from English to Spanish. I applied at the passport office here in lower Manhattan but did not receive any offers. I guess they know I will have two more years of school and they know I will be going back school and they would be minus an employee. Well, don't worry Sara, after school graduation I am sure you will find a really good job. I am getting hungry. I will make us a sandwich, OK? Yes, Marie, I am getting hungry too.

Tomorrow I am going to visit Granny, would you like to come with me? Yes, Marie, it has been quite a while since I have seen her, how is she doing? She is just fine and I am glad to stay with her while I'm going to NYU. Granny's home is just a few blocks from school and we enjoy each other company. She has shown me all the old photographs from when my dad was little and some relatives that are no longer around. It is funny to see the old fashions and how things were some fifty years ago. My grandfather passed away before I was born and I never knew him. My dad looks just like grandpa. When we visit Granny, I will ask her to show you our family photographs; some of these go away back to the 1920s. That will be cool to see, Marie! Yes, it will be a fun day. Maybe we can spend the weekend with her. I will have to ask Mom to call Granny when she gets home. I think my parents have plans for this weekend anyway! Travis sent them two tickets to Saturday's game, so I will be at my Granny's Saturday and Sunday.

Great idea, I am sure my mom will say it is "OK" for this weekend. I am ready to leave now. Your mom should be home shortly; see you on Saturday. A few minutes later Barbara arrived from work and Marie met her mom at the door. "Hi, Mom" did you have a nice day at work? It was fair, we were short-handed again and I have a lot to do". Tomorrow is the end of the week, so I guess they will all show up for the payday. Marie, did you and Sara enjoy the day together? Yes, mom, we had a great day and I was wondering if she can stay over the weekend at Granny's while you and Dad go see the ballgame, sounds like a great idea Marie but I will have to call Granny and ask if she would not mind the both of you for the weekend! Would you please call her and find out so I can let Sara know? Yes Marie, just give me ten minutes to change into something comfortable. Barbara called Granny and asked if she would not mind having Marie and her best friend Sara stay overnight Saturday and we will pick them up Sunday afternoon? Yes, of course, Barbara, I will enjoy their company for the weekend. How is Travis? He is fine and doing well at Yankee Stadium he always sends his love to Granny. We have two tickets to his game Saturday and we don't want to leave Marie home alone and I thought you would like company this weekend and have the girls stay with you! Yes, Barbara, I will love to have them stay over this weekend so I will not be alone and we can enjoy "chatting" and passing the time together. "Great Mom, I will have no worry about Marie being at the house alone while we go to the game this Saturday night, Thanks Mom". Marie said, "Thank you Granny". Mom this will be a great weekend! Do you need some help preparing dinner Mom? No, Marie, I was just making a tuna casserole for tonight, it will not take long. Thanks. I will just pack my overnight bag to take to Granny's and I am going to call Sara and let her know about our weekend. Marie contacted Sara and let her know that Granny said it is "OK" for this weekend and would love our company to keep her busy.

Dad will be home in a half-hour so I am getting into a hot shower and ready for the evening. Marie, would you please turn off the stove in five minutes? "OK, Mom". About ten minutes later her Dad arrived home from work, walked into the kitchen and asked Marie "what's cooking" I am starving! I was told to drain the macaroni and place it into the tuna mix and dinner will be ready. Where is Mom? She's getting changed for evening dad. How as your day? I have a really hectic day; I was too busy the entire day. How was your day, Marie? "Great" my friend Sara spent the day with me here at home and we talked all day about school and what we have to look forward to in the years ahead. Hi Barbara, you sure are looking good! I'm so hungry tonight because I did not even have time for lunch for today. "Smells good – dig in"

Dad, you are both going to the stadium Saturday for Travis's game, and Sara and I will spend the weekend at Granny's house. We called her and she said it will be nice to have company all day Saturday and Sunday. Do you think you can drive us to Granny's before you leave for the game? No problem with that has, Sara, be ready by 11:30 AM and I will take both of you to Granny's. I am sure you all will have a great weekend.

The Weekend at Granny's

Saturday morning arrived and Marie helped her mom make breakfast and they all enjoyed French toast, some OJ and coffee. I am calling Sara and let her know to be ready by 11:30 am. We will have a great time at Granny's. Dad stopped at the donut shop and bought a dozen of Granny's favorite fruit-filled donuts for us to have.

They arrived at Granny's and dad was happy to be able to find a parking space. Kids-grab your overnight cases I think I'll come in and see Granny too. They rang the doorbell and she let everyone in. Bob said; "I smell some of those homemade cookies do you have some for Travis"? Of course, Bob, I would not let Travis not get his favorite Granny's cookies! Girl, you can take your cases in the spare room and come have some cookies. Sara, how are you doing in school? "Not bad Granny" but it is a lot of work. I have spent hours of reading every night. I guess it is like they say "the more you read, the more you learn." It will all pay off the long run! Mom. "what time do you want to get these two girls out of your hair Sunday?" Bob, tell Barbara you two are invited to have Sunday dinner about 3:00 PM. To give Barbara a kitchen break, OK? The box of cookies is for Travis and give him my love. Thanks, mom I am sure he would appreciate it very much; see you Sunday, Bye". Do not forget the box of cookies for Travis and give him my love.

Granny, I told Sara about your photos that date back to 1920; You think she can look through your albums? "Yes Marie, you can take them from the china cabinet." Thanks, Granny! Sara viewed the photos page-by-page and opened every envelope that was also filled with pictures of Travis and myself from the day we were born, every birthday and every holiday we had together with the rest of the family members. Sara saw photographs of Granny and Grandpa from their wedding day and of my dad when he was born till his graduation and wedding to mom.

Sara is enjoying the photograph albums that Granny has taken out for her to see. We had some laughs on their old fashion styles. While we were enjoying the day, my grandmother was in the kitchen cooking dinner for us. We started watching out TV shows and Granny called us to come and eat. She made her special home-made vegetable soup and some fried chicken and some broccoli with cheese. This was a very delicious meal and we all enjoyed Granny's favorite fried chicken. She also brought a dish full of cookies which we all love. There is nothing like Granny's cookies with a glass of milk. Sara thanked her for the delicious meal. We helped clean-off the table and washed the dishes while Granny put the leftovers in her refrigerator. I told Granny it is time for her to watch TV and relax for the rest of the night. Sara and I are going to get changed into our pajamas and also watch some TV. We had a great "fun day" and it was the first time we could have each other's company for the whole weekend. I hope mom and dad are enjoying the ballgame at the stadium. This is the first time they went out without me tagging along. There is a movie starting at 8:00 PM, will it be OK to watch I Granny? "Yes, but I think I will clean up and get to bed soon". It seems that the older you get the more sleep our body needs! Enjoy the movie girls. I am turning in.

Marie turned the TV channel to the "Yes" channel to see how N.Y. Yankees were doing at their game; the score was 5 to 3 in their favor! She asked Sara if she would not mind watching an inning or two so she could get a glimpse at Travis at-bat. Go ahead Marie, I would love to see him play too. They watched the 7th inning and it was Travis' turn to bat. He had a man on base and he came up with a double, now the Yankees have a man on third and Travis on second base and he is hoping the next batter can get a hit to score two more runs. The batter got a hit and sent the two base runners' home and this made the score seven to three, Yankees favor. Marie said, "Now we go back to the movie". I guess my dad and mom are jumping for joy and feel that the Yankees can win this game easily. I am not a big sports fan, but I like to see Travis play whenever I can. Sara said, "he is doing well and looks like he is enjoying his work". I hope that after we graduate college, we can find a job to enjoy going to work as

Travis does! I am hoping that he improves at his game so that he will sign a big money contract the next time he signs up again. Dad is really proud of Travis and mom too is enjoying his success. Once the movie ended the girls went to sleep. The next day was Sunday and Granny likes to attend church when she has someone to walk with her. I guess she will ask us to go with her in the morning. Granny goes to bed early and rises early so we best get some sleep. The next morning, the great smell of breakfast woke the girls up and Granny did not have to call them to get out of bed. The girls stepped into the kitchen and found a breakfast feast on the table; there was scrambled eggs, toast, bacon, juice and chocolate milk ready for the girls. "Did everyone sleep well?" Yes Granny, we went to bed right after the movie was over. Would you girls like to attend church with me this morning? There will be an 11:00 AM mass.

I would like to leave by 10:30 AM; is that "OK" with you girls? We will be ready to go Granny. Thanks for breakfast Mrs. Smith; it was delicious! We had a great weekend with you Granny! When we get back home from church, I will call Dad and see when he will pick us up to go back home. Then Marie called home after church and asked her dad when they will come? Her dad thought they would take everyone out to dinner at about four o'clock. I would like to ask granny to join; will you please have her come to the telephone so I could ask her to join us! Hi Mom, would like to come out with us for dinner about four? Well, Bob if you don't mind, I feel tired and would rather stay home, "OK Mom" I will come about four to get the girls. Love you, see you later. Bob told Barbara about what his mom decided; She thought maybe they would drop off a dinner for her to have so she would not have to cook for herself tonight! I will tell her when we go pick up the girls or I think I will stop at the delicatessen and get her a delicious corned beef on rye and a cup of chicken noodle soup that is her favorite sandwich! Bob did that and Granny really appreciated his thoughtfulness. The girls were packed and ready to go. They thanked granny for a great weekend and gave her a big hug and kiss. See you during the week granny. Bye girls enjoy your meal.

How did Travis do on Saturday's game, Dad? Just great Marie, he has really improved quite a lot. He is also getting some good batting. He got two hits out of four times at bat and that was pretty good. Travis said he would come and visit on Wednesday which is the day of "No game" so he will spend it with us. He also wanted to see granny. Wednesday came around and Travis stopped at his grandmother's home first. She was glad to have his visit and asked him to have lunch with her.

Travis accepted her invite and enjoyed spending some time with her. Granny knew he was coming so she baked his favorite cookies and gave him some to take home. I heard from your dad about the game and he was thrilled with your improvement and those two hits you got during the game; I'm really glad you are doing well, love you! Thanks, Granny! It is three o'clock so I know Mom will be at home. I am headed there for a short visit too. I have to talk to Dad and Mom – I have a surprise for them I will see you again soon. Thanks for the cookies Granny.

Travis left and headed home to see his mom and sister and will have to wait until his dad came home from work to tell them the "good news"! In the meanwhile, he visited with his mom and Marie. So-Marie how are you doing at college? I would have to say that all my hard work at studying is paying off; I am doing really well and my grades are showing it too. Travis was getting anxious as the time went on and as soon as his dad walked in; he told him he had to talk to everyone right now. Mom, Dad come sit at the table. I have something to show all of you. He reached into his jacket pocket and pulled out a letter. This is it – I have been signed up with a three-year contract as the Yankee's short-stop player with a good size of money! This is for your real dad and I am very happy about it. This will mean that you do not have to worry about the college tuition is going to be paid! Dad, I will take care of all of Marie's school fees from now on. I am pleased with Marie's outstanding grades and I know she will complete her education and become the Architectural Engineer that she wants to achieve. I am more than happy to be able to do this for us all. His dad was speechless and his mom was drying the tears of joy for Marie and Travis said he is just glad to be able to do this for

Marie. OK – well let's eat. I have to get back home and get enough rest for the next day's game. Travis was thanked by his parents and Marie too.

Mom told Travis she is making his favorite dinner so he would not miss his roast beef, mashed potatoes, and vegetables which he loves so much. Bob and Travis were in the living room having a chat and I am sure Travis is like what he is saying because they both had big smiles on their faces and enjoying their time together. Bob and Travis had a great time and worked up a tremendous appetite for mom's delicious dinner. "Time to eat guys" was the welcomed call to the table. Bob said, "I think we have to pray a word of thanks for all the good happenings of the day." Amen. This was a very pleasant surprise and the best day of our lives so far.

Travis enjoyed his dinner and now it was time to get home. Dad, Mom, and Marie all hugged him and thanked him for his gift to Marie and the whole family! Be careful driving home and have a great game tomorrow Travis! Call us and let us know you have gotten home safely!

The phone rang about one hour after Travis left and he said – "it is only me" I am home – love you all.

Mom and Bob could relax now and get to sleep for the next day's work schedule. Marie told her parents she was thankful of Travis' gift to the family and now they take it easy for the next few years.

It may sound like a good idea, but we still have the next three or four years to take into consideration, Marie. Goodnight everyone, love you all.

The next morning came soon enough and Barbara was in the kitchen and making breakfast and lunch for Bob and Marie slept in for some extra rest. Mom left her the breakfast, dad left for work and mom and getting herself ready to go.

Three Years Later

Many changes will be happening for the Smith family.

Travis will be up to being offered a new contract.

Marie will be finishing four years of college. She will be out on the market seeking employment in Engineering.

Travis has a girlfriend and is thinking to become engaged to his girlfriend of two years. The family likes Malissa and thinks she is a wonderful girl. She lives at her parents' home not too far from Travis' home. She is employed by CBS in the advertising department in New York City,

Now, as the years go past, all these changes are normal circumstances. It is a pleasant feeling when all goes well and the family can enjoy their children's success.

Travis has made his dream come true and his career can only get better as the years go by.

Marie should not have a problem in getting employment in her field of study and she too has accomplished her dream and is looking forward to being placed in some big company in New York City as an Architectural Engineer. Granny is very proud of her grandchildren. Now she feels her son Bob and Barbara can start making plans for their retirement.

The motto of this story has proved that; "if you have a "dream" and pursue it till you achieve it you will be sitting on top of the world and have a great sense of accomplishment." Travis and Marie have done this and are extremely happy with their choices made for the future.

Best of luck to all future little Dreamers.

www.ingramcontent.com/pod-product-compliance
Lightning Source LLC
Chambersburg PA
CBHW050906120626
46554CB00003B/1041